THE TECHNIQUE OF MAHA YOGA

(SELF-ENQUIRY)

Culled from
TALKS WITH SRI RAMANA MAHARSHI
and arranged in Order of Sequence for
purposes of Practice

by
N. R. NARAYANA AIYER
(Sri Ramanasramam)

Sri Ramanasramam
Tiruvannamalai
2012

First Edition, 1962
Second Edition
(published by Ramana Kendra, Chennai), 1984
Third Edition, 1996
Fourth Edition, 2012 - 1000 Copies

CC No: 1159

ISBN: 978-81-8288-152-5

Price: ₹ 50/-

Published by

President
Sri Ramanasramam
Tiruvannamalai 606 603
Tamil Nadu, INDIA
Tel: 91-4175-237200/+919244937292
Email: ashram@sriramanamaharshi.org
Website: www.sriramanamaharshi.org

Printed by

Prism Art Press
Chennai - 600 014
India

INTRODUCTION

The author of this short work had sat at the feet of the foremost sage of the age, Sri Ramana Maharshi, for several years, in order to learn his sublime teachings. During this period he was and still is submitting himself to the strict discipline of spiritual life and regular practice.

Here in the manner of guiding the aspirants, the author is literally recording his own experience in this field in order to safeguard them against mistaking ideas and concepts for experience. To help them overcome some of the hurdles in this spiritual path, a few important *sadhanas* — such as *japa*, regulation of breath, regulated sleep, regular practice and its method — are all dealt with in their proper places. Passages dealing with *vasanas* and different *Samadhis* are interesting as well as illuminating. The statements are supported by some of the highest authorities and the experiences of great sages past and present.

This book will be highly useful for the aspirants in the *Jnana marga* — more especially in that of *vichara*.

SWAMI RAMANANANDA SARASWATHI

Sri Ramanasramam
Tiruvannamalai
25th March 1962

PREFACE

Though for some time there was an inner urge to collect the essential features of the practice of MAHA YOGA from the various 'talks' of Sri Bhagavan and concatenate them for purposes of practice for intending aspirants, there was also a certain amount of diffidence to do it, as it would be treading on virgin ground. Somehow the former urge got the better of the latter complex.

The whole range of *sadhana*, found scattered in the various 'talks', did need an arrangement. The readers and reviewers of the Asramam publications pointed out this want. Hence this treatise.

As Sri Bhagavan's method of Maha Yoga and its treatment is original and is not had in any Vedantic books in such detail, certain portions of the book as under *'vasanas'* and 'stillness' may be found to suffer from repetition; but such repetition was considered essential to bring home to the aspirant their importance in practice.

Again, in a compilation of this nature, where effort is made to reproduce, in his own words, Sri Bhagavan's teachings, which at times, covered the whole range of the Yoga in a few connected sentences, defects, due to repetition and inappropriateness of place are inevitable and the presentation on that account may not be happy. The indulgent reader must overlook these defects.

As it was noticed in the *Talks*, that several visitors enquired of Sri Bhagavan as to how Self-enquiry should be practised and as several aspirants must be groping in the dark as to how it should be done, the author thought it would be useful for earnest seekers, if he delineated the method he adopted from 1942 and which he found by experience to yield results. In 28th and 29th verses of *Ulladu Narpadu* (*Truth Revealed*) only, Sri Bhagavan has cryptically indicated the method of the *sadhana*. As any new aspirant trying to practise it, all at once, as laid down therein may find it hard to adopt it, the steps were graduated to facilitate the practice. It will be found that the steps the author indicated in Chap. II lead the aspirant gradually to the methods mentioned in those verses (*vide* Appendix).

It was also considered necessary to retail the experiences to show the effect of the *sadhana* during its progress. The experience of everyone may not be always on all fours with the author's, as it depends on the previous *samskaras* of each individual and one need not feel despondent if the experiences are not identical.

AUTHOR

PREFACE TO THE SECOND EDITION

Late Sri N. R. Narayana Aiyer was a long-standing devotee of Sri Bhagavan Ramana Maharshi. The book *Technique of Maha Yoga* written by him was first published by Sri Ramanasramam in 1962. This edition has run out of stock. As there is demand for copies of the book from devotees from India and abroad, the Ramanakendra, Madras, has decided to reprint the book for which permission has been obtained from The President, Sri Ramanasramam.

There is a bigger book entitled *Maha Yoga* by 'Who' published by Sri Ramanasramam, which deals with Bhagavan's philosophy based on *Ulladu Narpadu*, which is an authoritative treatise on Bhagavan's Teachings.

This book describes the techniques of *Vichara marga*, the Quest of the Self, based on the experiences of the writer. It will be found useful for earnest aspirants to practise the Path of Enquiry.

Madras
January 1, 1984

K. K. NAMBIAR
Chairman,
Ramanakendra,
Madras

DEDICATION

HUMBLY DEDICATED TO
BHAGAVAN SRI RAMANA,
THE ALL PERVADING SUPREME SPIRIT
RESIDING IN THE HEART OF ALL
BEINGS AND WHO IS BEYOND
SPACE AND TIME.

CONTENTS

SRI RAMANA MAHARSHI

Born on 30th December 1879 at Tiruchuzhi, a small township in Ramnad District, in a brahmin family, Venkataraman, later reverently named Sri Ramana Maharshi, educated at Dindigul and Madurai up to matriculation standard, left his home unnoticed for Tiruvannamalai on 31st August 1896 in his seventeenth year and continued to stay there till he attained his *mahasamadhi* on 14th April 1950.

It would be interesting to study the outstanding features of his spiritual life. While yet in his eleventh year, he was having *samadhi* for sleep, which he modestly called "heavy sleep", and he could not be roused from his 'torpor' except by giving him a violent shake. He was also subject to fits of half-awake sleep which most *jivanmuktas* experience prior to Self-realisation. So from his early boyhood he effortlessly attained a state which seemed to be a prelude to the dawn of realisation which he had in one sitting when he dramatised death for a few minutes. In that short period of minutes he crossed the rubicon and was thrown into the lap of gods. Thereafter he had no control over his actions. He was a passive instrument of the great power, the Self, which he calls 'Arunachala' in the *Five Hymns to Arunachala*. His mind was, as it were, held in close embrace by the Self till it became extinct and was transformed into 'That'. A study of the hymns leads us to the above conclusion.

A *jivanmukta* after realisation develops moment after moment on the spiritual side *vide* Chapter XI, Verses 18 and 19 *Ramana Gita,* and the Maharshi, living for 54 years after realisation, attained Godhead and if people did not realise this, it was the *Maya* that was shrouding them which prevented people recognising his greatness, just as Lord Krishna was not recognised as a great incarnation except by the wise in those days.

The *Bhagavad Gita* and *Yoga Vasishta* say that those that are in the path of yoga with certain attainments at death continue from where they left off in their subsequent birth. Apparently, in his previous birth he must have finished his fourth *jnana bhumika* of *Sattvapatti*. This should have ordinarily given him liberation in that birth; but strong desires at death to be reborn and be a great living teacher and be an instrument for emancipating people must have been the cause of the present birth. His involuntary, unrecognised *samadhi* in his boyhood and his effortless Self-realisation and his prayers in the temple at Madurai that he must be like the Tamil saints point to our above conclusion.

His sudden interest in Arunachala when casually mentioned; his departure for Tiruvannamalai without any apparent premeditation of his destination and his frequent mention of his knowing every inch of the hill and his mention in one of the *Talks*, "I was indeed fortunate that I never took to philosophy. Had I taken to it I would probably be nowhere — always in confusion. My *purva vasanas* directly took me to the enquiry 'Who am I?';" and his effortless command of classical Tamil at a very young age, are all pointers to his stay, attainments and *tapas* in Arunachala in his previous birth.

At the very early age of 20 or less he was able to give clear instructions to earnest aspirants in *jnana yoga*. Such questions and answers were collected together and were printed in pamphlet form in later years with the titles of *Who am I?, Spiritual Instructions* and *Catechism of Self Enquiry*.

Self enquiry of 'Who am I?' which is slightly touched upon in *Yoga Vasishta, Viveka Chudamani* and other *Vedanta* scriptures is given a shape in the several pamphlets and talks. It is recommended as a panacea for all material and mental sufferings. It is also recommended for eradicating *vasanas*, destroying the mind and becoming a *jnani*.

Sri Bhagavan said that the advent of a world teacher is in keeping with the times and the maturity of the people wanting instructions to benefit by them. The various "Talks", recorded in the three volumes, indicate the degrees of ripeness of the questioners.

The Talks recorded in Vol. II of the *Maharshi's Gospel* indicate the shrewdness, understanding and capacity to draw out great truths for the guidance of *sadhakas* by the questioner, Mr. M. Frydman, a Pole. These works are a valuable gift to posterity.

Sri Bhagavan was averse to writing any books and the wonder is that books are published by his personal devotees and there seems to be no end of them for some time to come.

The advent of a *Jnani* of such stature occurs once in several centuries. They are styled *Aadhikarika Purushas*, (authorised agents to revivify a decadent school of thought and to guide the world in spiritual matters); and Sri Bhagavan seems to have admitted he is one of them to one of his close devotees.

Rare indeed is the luck of those who gave birth to such a great soul and those that descended in his family. *Varaha Upanishad* says that descendents of such a person for 101 generations get release from bondage effortlessly. What indeed must be the luck and *purvapunnya* of those who had the great luck of his *darsan* and of sitting at his feet day in and day out!

Ribhu Gita says the *darsan* of a *jnani* has the effect of a bath in the holy waters. *Varaha Upanishad* says that the sins of those that have *darsan* of a *Brahmavit* are destroyed and if such a sage turns his gracious glance on anyone, sins of his previous lives are destroyed. The mere stay in a *jnani's* presence is a spiritual bath. His mere existence radiates spiritual influence the world over in all directions and those who were receptive by being introverted received as much as they were fit for. Just as the sun, as soon as it rises, develops the bud and makes the developed bud to blossom, so also spiritually minded *sadhakas* developed themselves by such radiations when they were in-turned. Hence the spate of *Jivanmuktas* during and subsequent to his time namely, Sri Ma Anandamayi, Sri Aurobindo, Swami Ramadas, Swami Sivananda, late Sankaracharya of Sringeri, who passed away in 1959, Sri Sankaracharya of Kamakoti Peetam, late Seshadriswami of Tiruvannamalai, late Kuttalam Mowna Swami, late Sendamangalam Swami, late Eswara Swami of Tiruvannamalai, Sri Jnanananda Swami of Tapovanam, late Sri Purushottamanandaji of Hrishikesh who passed away in 1961, late Mr. H. T. Hamblin of Sussex, and many more of whom we may not know.

Many ripe visitors even in their first hours of stay experienced *samadhi*. *Samadhi* results on account of mental stillness, Sri Bhagavan's proximity in his state of mental *mowna* was enough to quell the thoughts of those ripe souls present. His gaze, when directed with intent on any person, raked up that person's dormant spiritual awareness and gave it a fillip to get active. While normally the onlooker would be thinking he is simply gazing at a person, he, by his look, would be giving instructions and the recipient unmistakably understood the import conveyed by his gaze. There was no mistaking the meaning.

Sri Bhagavan once said, "The cosmic mind manifesting in some rare sage is able to effect the linkage of the individual mind with the inner Self." Sri Bhagavan had this unique power.

While it is the common talk that he did not initiate any, he did really initiate some. Mr. Paul Brunton could not have got into *samadhi* but for his initiation by the gaze. He has related his experiences during his *samadhi*.

One other European was Mr. Grant Duff. When he entered the hall and sat down, Sri Bhagavan directed his gaze on him, for over an hour, in spite of the dinner bell and did not leave the hall till he had finished with him.

The third day after my settling down at Tiruvannamalai, soon after I prostrated before him and sat down, he indicated me to close my eyes by closing his eyes and, when I passively closed my eyes, within five minutes I was unaware of what was happening for nearly half an hour after which I was released from his mental grip. This continued for nearly a month. Within a fortnight, I was involuntarily repeating "Who am I?".

When my wife visited him a week after settling down in the home, he did the same with her and whenever she visited him, thus laying the foundation for her *sadhana*. How many others were similarly initiated is known to him and themselves only. To say that he did not initiate anyone is incorrect.

If by the presence in his proximity one's thoughts could be quelled and if by his gaze one's mind could be steadily fixed on one's heart, it is not to be wondered at, that by his touch with intent on his mother he was able to destroy all her remnant *vasanas* and release her from the cycle of births thus giving liberation.

On his *Jayanthi* and *Mahapuja* of his mother he used to send out his gracious influence to his absent devotees at about 10-30 a.m. prior to the dinner and once while in my village about 150 miles away, on a *Jayanthi* day, I unmistakably felt the influence during my usual *sadhana* at the time, unanticipated. In subsequent years when, at Tiruvannamalai, I noticed him grim with concentration at that particular time, I was able to connect it with my experience. Later one day when I related to him this experience he showed interest and eagerness to hear it, probably to know the effect of his concentrated message on his distant absentee devotees.

He used to insist on the poor waiting outside to be first fed prior to his taking food. Similarly on *Jayanthi* and *Mahapuja* days he would not go for dinner till he learnt that poor-feeding had started. On *Karthika Deepam* festival days he used to say, "We do not know in what form the *siddhas* that inhabit this hill come here. They must be fed first."

Though he did not apparently show interest in the construction of the temple, a year before his *mahasamadhi* he directed that the temple should be completed quickly. While, previously, the construction was going at snail's pace it took giant strides with hundreds of labourers engaged daily and the *Sarvadhikari* was hard put to it often to meet the daily wages of the labourers. Nothing, according to Sri Bhagavan, should be left incomplete.

On the midnight, previous to the Consecration day, he, with the sculptor-architect, *Sarvadhikari*, Mr. Chadwick and a few others, entered the temple and touched the various seats where the deities were to be installed, by a circular movement of the hand, thus consecrating them himself. Ceremonial rituals and consecration were performed by scores of learned Brahmin pundits in the most orthodox style on the Consecration day. Crowds numbering a lakh and over from far and near and mostly from the surrounding villages witnessed the function.

During the last decade of his life, though the influx of foreign visitors was comparatively small, due to the aftermath of the war, the Indian element was so great that he had to shift to more commodious places.

It was noteworthy that during this period many maharajas with their consorts, governors of States, ministers and administrators and noteworthy people visited him and paid homage.

He frequently expressed that he was beyond space and time, that is, he is eternal and could be got at now or 100 years hence or till eternity and from anywhere irrespective of place.

To corroborate this, it would be interesting to mention the following:— An English lady asked the Asramam by letter for spiritual instruction in 1956, that is, six years after Sri Bhagavan's *mahasamadhi*. She was asked to repeat the *japa* of "*Om Namo Bhagavate Sri Ramanaya*" which she said she was sedulously repeating. A couple of years later, she wrote to say that some voice immanent in her was questioning "Who is praying?" "Who is asking?" and such like questions all revolving on "Who am I?". She was directed to the path of Self-enquiry. From this, it would be clear that earnest aspirants get his guidance irrespective of time and place.

During the fag end of his life when people learnt that he was in poor health, on account of sarcoma, from which he was suffering, devotees in large numbers from far and near as also other people from the town and surrounding villages were visiting the Asramam in large numbers and the forty feet road was always crowded to capacity. To the last day he was giving *darsan* to all the people who filed past him.

When he attained *mahasamadhi* at 8-47 p.m. on 14th April 1950 a big bright flaming star was noticed going towards the north. This was noticed even by people in Madras and other surrounding places.

His remains were interred the next evening in the Asramam itself alongside the temple but separate from it. A small temporary shrine was erected over it and a *Siva Linga* installed and *poojas* to it according to Hindu *agamas* are performed daily morning and evening. A permanent shrine is under way.

People who have lost their peace of mind, on account of the loss of their dear ones, have been known to regain their former composure by sitting in the proximity of the shrine for a few hours a day for a few days.

The sanctity of Arunachala added to the powerful radiation emanating from the shrine and the peaceful atmosphere of the place contribute to easy concentration, so that new *sadhakas* from other places were immediately struck by it and have stayed for a few years for developing their *sadhana*.

A good number of men and women who have been used to meditate there during Sri Bhagavan's time continue their *sadhana* there; and they are disinclined to leave the place and if they do, they feel like fish out of water eagerly wanting to come back.

Apart from the old devotees, persons from foreign countries and other provinces of India, who have not even seen Sri Bhagavan during his lifetime have come to stay for purpose of *sadhana* at great personal sacrifice.

Tiruvannamalai, by itself, is reputed as the hill that invites *jnana sadhakas* and many are the people who have attained liberation here. Lord Shiva ordained that "residence within a radius of thirty miles of the hill shall, by itself, be sufficient to burn off all defects and effect the union of the individual soul with the Supreme, even without initiation."

Sri Bhagavan used to express that there are several *siddha purushas* inhabiting the hill. Sri Parvathi Devi, Sages Gautama and Dhurvasa did *tapas* here in the olden days and their *ashramas* still exist.

The tomb of the mother of Sri Bhagavan which was housed in a small hut formed the nucleus of the present Sri Ramanasramam. Thereafter, Sri Bhagavan's hall, the *gosala* (cowshed), the *Vedapatasala* (Vedic school), the store room, the *pakasala* (kitchen and dining hall), *Vaidyasala* (hospital) and later the temple, successively came into existence spontaneously without any effort or desire on the part of Sri Bhagavan.

At present solicitude of the management for the convenience of the devotees and the *sadhakas*, the arrangement for the accommodation and for boarding of casual visitors, high and low, and for those wanting to stay for longer periods for *sadhana*, the clean maintenance of the Asramam and the publication of books propagating Sri Bhagavan's teachings in the various Indian and foreign languages, all point to a healthy growth now, even within a dozen years of his *Mahasamadhi*.

Sri Sankaracharya of Kamakoti Peetam was said to remark that the greatness of the Asramam will be apparent fifty years hence. Whether it is a prophecy or wishful thinking of the carrier of this news, posterity alone can judge to what heights the Asramam has grown for the benefit of the world at large.

Chapter I

MAHA YOGA

INTRODUCTION

Caught in the vortex of the cycle of births and deaths transmigrating through eighty-four lakhs of species of animated beings, one evolves as a human being. Even then he has still the old strong animal instincts and is not capable of discriminating the good from the bad. When, as a result of suffering, the primitive man recognises a supreme power, prays to it to get over his suffering and the gracious Lord is pleased to relieve him of it, faith in the Lord is created and then through habit he worships God even though he may not have any suffering. Thus is paved the way for devotion. Later he utilises his devotion for getting the pleasures of the world and heaven, ignorant of the aim of human birth which is liberation from the cycle of births and deaths. This worship by *pooja*, later by singing praises, which, while in the beginning, is occasional, becomes frequent and later is continuous. He also has recourse to *japa* which is repetition to keep him in unceasing remembrance of God. When with

this supreme devotion all his actions are done in a spirit of dedication to God, the goddess of Self is pleased and directs him to the path of liberation.

Ribhu Gita says that only in those that have obtained Grace by worship and extreme devotion to Lord Siva is generated the belief in the oneness of all, and not in others.

In *Panchadasi, Dhyanadeepika*, it is said that he, who has in several previous births done motiveless actions dedicated to God[1], becoming ripe for Self-enquiry, is desirous of practising *Atma vichara* (Self-enquiry).

The *Bhagavad Gita* emphasizes motiveless action leading to *Jnana* and then to liberation.

Sri Bhagavan in the third verse of his *Upadesa Sara* says motiveless actions dedicated to God correct the individual's approach and direct him to the path of liberation. While previously his virtuous actions were motivated by a desire for heavens or better future births, the individual surrendering the fruits of his actions to God leaving no residue of such fruits to himself is forced into the *Jnana marga*. Once he dedicates his actions to God he gets into the habit of doing so, so that all his actions including his daily routine duties are done in a spirit of service to God. Even the maintenance of the family and the work therefore are done in the same spirit gradually

[1] For dedicating actions to God one has only to say at the end of actions "Lord, I surrender the fruits of these actions to you" or simply say "Brahmarpanam", meaning done in dedication to the Self.

resulting in detachment from the family also. Then it dawns in his mind, "How many parents, wives and children I must have had in my several previous births! Am I concerned with them now? The same will be the case with the present ones also." This detachment grows, which again leads to *vairagya* (dispassion) and *mumukshutva* (desire for liberation).

1. JNANA YOGA

In the *Jnana Yoga* there is the *dhyana marga* and there is the *vichara marga*, which Sri Bhagavan calls MAHA YOGA. The former deals with the meditation on one of the *Mahavakyas* "*Aham Brahmasmi*" (I am the Self). Sri Bhagavan recommends the MAHA YOGA as a more direct method for easy concentration of mind and consequent eradication of *vasanas* and extinction of the mind.

Sri Bhagavan tersely puts the whole scheme of Maha Yoga in *Vichara Sangraha* (Self-Enquiry) as follows:- By constant practice of enquiry is obtained the extinction of mind. This extinction is the ultimate result of all efforts. Those in this state never swerve from this position. *Mowna* or to remain still is this state. All *sadhanas* are for obtaining concentration of mind; for to think, to desire, to hate, etc., are all modifications of mind and cannot be the natural state of the Self. The mere immutable quiescent state of mind alone is one's natural state. Till this state of mental stillness gets firm, not to lose hold of the Self and not to

contaminate the mind with thoughts are the two essentials to be observed in the *sadhana*.

2. THE SEVEN STAGES OF JNANA YOGA

There are seven *Bhumikas* or stages in *Jnana Yoga*:- (1) *Subechcha*, (2) *Vicharana*, (3) *Tanumanasi*, (4) *Sattvapatti*, (5) *Asamsakthi*, (6) *Padharthabhavana*, (7) *Turiya*.

1. Dispassion for wife and children, *mumukshutva* (desire for liberation) and the desire that arises in one through sheer *vairagya* after resolving, "Shall I be ignorant? I will study the *jnana sastras* and seek the company of the wise," is termed *Subechcha*.

2. Association with the wise and the earnest and constant study of the various *jnana sastras* is *Vicharana*.

3. Absolute faith in the scriptures and in the teachings of the wise and the practice of the *sadhana* or meditation leading to the thinning of the mind and to the weakening of the hankering for sense objects is termed *Tanumanasi*.

4. The stage wherein having got indifferent to all sense objects by the practice of the above three stages the purified mind, getting ripe, gets fixed in the Heart is called *Sattvapatti*.

5. As a result of the practice of the four previous stages mind getting absorbed in the Heart manifesting pure *sattva guna* is termed *Asamsakthi*.

6. That stage wherein as a result of the practice of the above five stages one having found delight in *Atman* is not

conscious of internals and externals though before him and engages in actions only when impelled to do so is termed *Padarthabhavana*.

7. The stage wherein by exceedingly long practice in the above six stages one immoveably abides in *Atman* alone, having lost the experience of the distinction of the world, is termed *Turiya*.

3. GURU

God, Guru and the inner Self are the same.

It is stated in all the Hindu Scriptures that a Guru is always necessary. Ordinarily, anyone cannot start practice of *Jnana Yoga* without the aid of a Jnana Guru. *The Bhagavad Gita* IV. 34. states a *Brahma Jnani* alone can initiate one in *Brahma Jnana* or at least it implies that.

Bhagavan Sri Ramana in *Vichara-Sangraha* (Self-enquiry) says that as a result of motiveless actions in dedication to God done in several previous births, mind getting purified, an aspirant meets his Guru, gets *Upadesa* (instructions) from him, and by long, intense and incessant practice gets liberation.

Sometimes, in the case of a few earnest aspirants some great souls suggest that they hold in their heart the use of any emblem such as a photo or a figure of their chosen Guru, and to start the practice as mentioned in their teachings with great faith and devotion. The story of Ekalavya, the hunter, is cited as an instance.

When Dronacharya, the archery Guru of Arjuna, declined to take Ekalavya as his disciple in archery, Ekalavya instead of being discouraged made a figure of Dronacharya in the forest near his abode, worshipped the figure with great devotion as if it was the real embodiment of his Guru, and started practising archery in front of it and became an expert and an equal of Arjuna in archery.

Once when Arjuna and Dronacharya, with Arjuna's dog preceding them, were passing through the forest where Ekalavya was practising, Ekalavya aimed an arrow at the dog which, piercing through the face of the dog, got stuck up in its hind parts. The dog being hit ran towards its master who, seeing the dog in that condition, asked his master, "You taught me this kind of archery and said you had taught this to no one else. Here we see someone else also is an adept." Dronacharya said, "Let us proceed and see who this is."

When they came upon Ekalavya he fell prostrate before his Guru in bodily form with great trepidation. When, Dronacharya asked him who taught him archery, he pointed to the figure and said, "Yourself". As the master was nonplussed at finding a rival to Arjuna he asked Ekalavya, "Where is the Guru *dakshina* (offering)?" Ekalavya replied that he was prepared to give whatever was demanded. Dronacharya then demanded of him his right thumb and Ekalavya without the least hesitation drew his hunting knife, severed his right thumb and offered it to his Guru with great humility.

In the various *puranas* and stories of saints it is said that when the aspirant is ripe God arranges for him to meet a guru; and even a casual word uttered by the guru is treasured and acted upon, which leads the aspirant to liberation.

When Sage Thayumanavar was ripe, a teacher appeared before him and they were together for a short time. When up to the time of parting he was not given any instruction and was importuning him while leaving, the Guru said, "Keep quiet". The disciple considered it as his *upadesa* and practised 'keeping quiet', meaning mental quiescence. Anyone else would have taken the parting words as said in disgust to an importunate man; but in ripe Thayumanavar, it acted differently and he took those words as real *upadesa* and practised mental quiescence and became a great sage.

Again certain ripe souls having had the necessary *upadesa* in their previous birth and left their *sadhana* incomplete, start from where they left off and complete their *sadhana* without the aid of a personal Guru and obtain liberation.

Others again who in their previous lives have attained the maturity to look upon their Inner Self as their Guru and were getting their instructions therefrom needed no outer Guru and recognised their Inner Self as their Guru from the start. During their *sadhana* in the deep stillness of thought-free consciousness, the Inner Voice speaks and guides them. This also occurs in mature *sadhakas* when they lose personal contact with their Guru for any reason and they do not go about searching for a new Guru.

Sri Bhagavan, in reply to an American businessman's request for a message which he might treasure and carry with him when away from Sri Bhagavan said, "The Guru is not outside as you seem to think. He is inside you and is in fact the Self. Recognise this truth. Seek within you and find him there. Then you will have constant communion with him. The message is always there, It is never silent. It can never forsake you. Nor can you move away from the Guru."[2]

With the progress of *sadhana* in this Maha Yoga, one naturally develops the habit of looking upon the Inner Self as the Guru and his photo or any symbol loses its original significance thereafter. One's prayer, if any, is always directed to the Self within and one does not differentiate between God, Guru and the Self.

4. GRACE

Sri Bhagavan once said, "What is Grace? It is a function of God." Like the rays of the sun, Grace is always functioning; there is no moment when it is not; but it is dependent on the receptivity of the individual to partake of it. What contributes to the receptivity of Grace in the individual? It is *suddha chittham* (purified mind) caused by several factors, namely, love for fellow-humans and sympathy to human suffering resulting in charitable acts, pilgrimages, bath in holy waters, worship of God by singing praises of Him, *japa*, *pranayama*, meditation, etc. Like a schoolboy moving from a lower to a higher class by qualifying himself for it, this *chittha suddhi* of

---

[2] *Talks with Sri Ramana Maharshi,* Talk No. 503.

varying nature develops the spirituality of the individual, step by step, and Grace aids him by guiding him. Grace is very manifest, when there is *sraddha* (earnestness). With increase in *bhakti, japa*, and meditation, the individual becomes very receptive to Grace. He experiences it and attributes every good, material and spiritual, to this overshadowing Grace. This, in turn, induces absolute surrender and immediate rejection of any thought of conscious planning.

One engrossed totally in worldliness is impervious to Grace.

5. PRAYER

Devotees are of two kinds, namely *saguna upasakas* (devotees of god with form) and *nirguna upasakas* (devotees of god without form). Their devotion is termed *annya bhakthi* (devotion to god external to oneself) and *an-annya bhakthi* (devotion to god not external to oneself) respectively. *Saguna upasana* must precede *nirguna upasana*. The individual is not generally ripe enough straightaway to get into *nirguna upasana*. Constant repetition of praises or stotras of the chosen god which enrapture him, and remembrance of such god by frequent or constant appropriate *japa* are successive steps leading to *anannya bhakthi*.

Prayer is always resored to by *saguna upasakas*. India is studded with temples, the deities of which have been famous from ancient times for the grant of boons of devotees. Tirupati (Balaji), Palani, Madurai, Chidambaram and

Rameswaram in South India and numerous other places in the country attract devotees all the year round where vows are taken and solemnly fulfilled. Even today prayers of the devotees of these deities are granted in a measure more than desired or anticipated.

With the maturity of *saguna upasana*, the individual is automatically led into the *nirguna upasana* stage. With the cultivation of the worship of the Inner Self by meditation and later by the intensity of such meditation, communion with the Inner Self is established. Prayer, thereafter, seems superfluous for everything is done in the fullest measure for the *sadhaka* (practicant) unasked.

Lord Krishna says, "I take over the interests and welfare of those who worship me as their Inner Self" (B.G. IX 22). Though there is a deeper meaning for the verse, the above is sufficient here.

If any attempt is made by the *nirguna upasaka* in his advanced stage, to pray for anything for himself or his dear ones, he is foiled in his attempt; for just then the mind stands stock still, unable to formulate one word of prayer. When this frustration is experienced two or three times his prayer resolves into "Oh Lord! Let Thy will be done."

6. SLEEP

Sleep is sometimes considered as an obstacle to *sadhana*. While a *sadhaka* should not avoid sleep totally, he can gradually reduce the period to four or five hours daily without detriment to his health or *sadhana*. If his activities are totally taken away by circumstances or age, the normal period of six to eight hours is a little too much. If the *sadhaka* goes to sleep about eight or nine in the night and wakes up at about six, he should start waking up at five and then after a month at four and so on till the maximum of four or five hours is obtained utilising the early morning hours for meditation, when, one being fresh from sleep with the mind and body rested and the world outside quite still, it is very conducive to *sadhana*.

Bhagavan Sri Ramakrishna said that *bhogis* (debauchees), *rogis* (the sick) and *yogis* (*sadhakas*) don't sleep in the night. Remaining on four or five hours of sleep daily, one is condensing the full deep sleep period and feels none the worse for it and getting up after the period has a feeling of satiation just as one feels after a full meal. Occasionally when the system does want sleep it is better to let nature have its way. Anyhow utilising a good part of the still night for *sadhana*, the progress is very good and the *sadhaka* feels greatly encouraged by the result. Indeed, every improvement in one's *sadhana* and every spiritual experience are noticeable mainly in the early morning meditation.

Sleep can be used with great advantage by earnest aspirants for their *sadhana* either in *Bhakti* or *Jnana Yoga*. Just fifteen minutes prior to sleeping in his bed if he keeps repeating *japa mantra* or any verse in praise of his *Ishta*

Devatha (chosen deity) and goes to sleep with it in his lips, his subconscious mind takes it up and keeps repeating it throughout sleep and he wakes up with the *japa* or verse on his lips.

Similarly if the aspirant keeps repeating, 'Who am I?' with his mind on the Self, he is effortlessly aiding his *sadhana*; and those in *dhyana marga*, if they with *bhavana* (mental visualisation) keep repeating, "The all pervading *Atma* is myself alone," will find it to their advantage. Of course, in the last two cases sleep period will be a sort of trance or a mixture of wakefulness and sleep: but the *sadhaka* will be none the worse for it. Indeed, the sweetness of mind on waking up will be such that he would like to cultivate the practice.

7. JAPA

In the spiritual path, whether of devotion or *jnana*, the potency of *japa* and of its aid are very great and no aspirant can afford to get on with his *sadhana* without its aid as a support. In all religions, Christian, Buddhist, Islamic and Hindu, the aspirants have been noticed to be rolling their beads even while walking so that they may not break the continuity of their *japa*.

Valmiki, a hunter, became a highway robber and a murderer. Sage Narada divining his *purva punnya* wanted to initiate him in *Rama Nama Japa*. Being a great sinner in his current life he could not even pronounce "Rama". Since he was used to '*mara*' '*mara*' meaning 'kill', Narada asked him to repeat '*mara*' which when continuously uttered became 'Rama, Rama'. The robber was so intense in his repetition that he lost body-consciousness for years and an anthill grew up covering him. He got Self-realisation, became a great sage and a great poet, and the author of the original Sanskrit *Ramayana* in verses. Authors of subsequent *Ramayanas* in other languages took their material from this original book.

Thyaga Brahmam, the musician-saint of South India born in 1759 repeated Rama *mantra* several crores of times, became a poet and strung his poems to music. He lived on alms while going round the streets singing songs on Rama. He was much venerated. He attained Self-realisation only by *japa*. The Lord to prove his greatness to the world made him touch a dead body over which the relatives were wailing and the dead person was revived. This occurred during his pilgrimage to Tirupati.

Swami Ramadas of Kanhangad attained Self-realisation purely by repetition of Rama Nama.

Repetition of the name of the chosen deity when regularly practised for an hour in the morning and in the evening for a couple of months makes the person do it unconsciously even while at work and at odd moments. Later he gets a vision of the deity of his *japa*. Encouraged by this, he becomes more devoted to the *mantra* and keeps continuously uttering it. Later he unwittingly concentrates on the repetition, *i.e.*, hearing the mental articulation with the mental ear. This makes the mind merge in the source of the utterance, the Heart. Thus from the path of devotion he is unwittingly led to the path of *jnana*.

About 1946 Mr. and Mrs. Khanna of Kanpur with their children, ranging from two to seventeen years, were living for nearly three months near the Asramam, coming to the hall, mornings and evenings daily. At the time of parting Mrs. Khanna asked Sri Bhagavan what she should do in the spiritual path with so much on her hands pointing to her children. Sri Bhagavan benignly instructed her, "Repeat 'I', 'I', 'I', all the time, even while at work and read the pamphlet 'Who am I?' once a day. That's enough." How simple an instruction to understand, how easy to follow and how profound in effect when followed. Repetition of 'I' 'I' when at work keeps thoughts away. When free from work the repetition makes the mind involuntarily go to the source of 'I', where the mind rests. The mind thus gradually gets extinct, and Self-realisation results. In the beginning, while reading 'Who am I?' the person understands the superficial meaning, but with the progress of repetition resulting in meditation and spiritual unfoldment, the deeper meaning of the substance of the book gets clearer and helps the *sadhaka*.

Similarly with the repetition of "Who am I?". Sri Bhagavan says of all the *japas*, 'Who am I?' is the best.[3]

Swami Ramadas says *japa* should not be mere lip work, but every atom of the whole body must throb

[3] *Talks with Sri Ramana Maharshi*, Talk No. 72.

with it. Saint Tukaram used to utter Ram Nam always, even while answering calls of nature. When a Brahmin priest saw this and scolded him for this, he stopped the repetition. Immediately every pore of his body started uttering it and caused a din. Such must be the intensity of *japa*.

Incidentally, busy persons after retirement from occupation, confronted with emptiness of life become mental wrecks. To occupy their time, they take to radio-listening, newspapers, politics, and so on. Some even take to reading religious books and writing articles for journals, etc., and yet they find a voidness in their life which they are not able to figure out. If people, even in their late forties, take to *japa sadhana* for half an hour daily in the mornings and evenings, they would, by the time they retire, have reached a stage when they will be anxiously looking forward to the day of retirement, so that they may fully occupy themselves in this *japa sadhana*. Even starting after retirement if a person resolutely employs his time in *japa* he would be leading a good spiritual life and would at least set an example to the family and those that come in contact with him.

8. MAHA YOGA

In Maha Yoga the individual feels he has got out of his primal state of oneness with the Self and wants to regain his natural state. What is this original or natural state? It is the egoless thought-free state of bliss. We have a glimpse of its experience during sleep, when we feel the blissful state, for in that state we are free from thoughts. And what is our present state? It is the state of *ajnana* or ignorance, full of ego sense and mental *vrittis* (thought forms). These thought waves, pleasant and unpleasant, cause us ultimate misery and continued *samsara*, the cycle of births and deaths. What are these thought waves and how are they caused and how are they overcome? These thought waves are due to *vasanas*.

9. VASANAS

When a thought occurs and passes off, it leaves an impression on the subconscious mind; when the same thought occurs again it underscores the original impression and if the same thought frequently occurs, the impression becomes deeper and when it gets a good hold, the thought recurs uninvited. These impressions recorded in the subconscious mind take a seed form and sink deep into the heart at the time of death and do not perish; they are carried over to the next birth as *vasanas* or *purva samskaras* or latent tendencies. They, in right time, sprout forth from the Heart.[4] The Self safeguards these *vasanas* in its closest proximity within itself, the Heart, just as a miser keeps his valued possessions within himself and never out of contact.[5] When a *vasana* is released from the

[4] *Talks with Sri Ramana Maharshi*, T. 108.

[5] *Ibid.*, T. 402.

Heart and comes to play, it is associated with the light of the Self and the person is said to think. It passes from the heart to the brain and on its way the transformed thought grows more and more until it holds sway all alone; for the time being all other *vasanas* are held in abeyance. When the original *vasana* has spent itself, another more insistent and waiting *vasana* takes the field and occupies the mind and so on.[6]

Reverting to thought impressions, it must be stated they determine the character of the individual. They make or mar a spiritual man. When thoughts of God and of kindness to fellow-beings engage the mind and predominate, they elevate him and gradually lead him to ripeness for spiritual discipline and later to eminence in the spiritual field.

Contrarily, selfishness, indifference to the sufferings of others, envy, egotism, anger and hatred lead to vindictiveness, cruelty, and the primitive savagery of man. Persons as they advance in age, if they are not careful of their thoughts and persist in their old, crooked, cunning and lustful ways, become cantankerous and insufferable and people avoid them. They suffer hell even while alive. If these evil *samskaras* are carried over to the next birth, it is not hard to divine the nature of the child and God in His wisdom places him in families and environments suitable to his nature (B. G. XVI).

The only easy remedy to get over these evil propensities is recourse to *japa* and constant remembrance of God.

---

[6] *Ibid.*, T. 616.

These will certainly sublimate all evil tendencies and change the individual, completely. There need be no doubt about this.

In *jagrat* (waking) state when a man is idle his mind is kept engaged by these latent *vasanas*. The mind is never idle. It is like a running mill wanting grist to grind and the *vasanas* supply it.

In the *Arunachala Ashtaka* or the *Eight Verses on Arunachala*, in the sixth verse addressing the Heart Sri Bhagavan says, "Thou art Thyself, the one Being ever aware as the Self-luminous Heart. In Thee, there is a mysterious Power which without Thee is nothing. From it proceeds the phantom of the mind emitting its latent dark subtle mists, which, illumined by Thy light of consciousness reflected on them, appear within as thoughts whirling in the vortices of *prarabdha,* later developing into the psychic worlds and, projected outwardly, as the material world transformed into concrete objects which are magnified by the outgoing senses and move like pictures in the cinema show. Visible or invisible, Oh hill of Grace, without Thee they are nothing!"

Incidentally this gives the key to the saying that all manifestations including world, body, etc., are objectified thoughts and are therefore not real.

So these *vasanas* transformed into thoughts obstruct the aspirant during meditation. So long as *vasanas* remain and are not completely destroyed realisation cannot be achieved. These *vasanas* can be obliterated only by concentration on that which is free from *vasanas*, that is, the Heart.[7]

The seekers aim should be to drain away the *vasanas* from the Heart and let no reflection obstruct the light of Consciousness. This is achieved by the search for the source of the ego.[8] This is the direct method. The state free from *vasanas* is the primal state and the eternal state of purity.

On another occasion speaking about the scheme of liberation Sri Bhagavan said, "Just as water in the pot reflects the enormous sun within the narrow limits of the pot, even so the *vasanas* or latent tendencies of the individual acting as the reflecting medium, catch the all pervading light of Consciousness arising from the heart and present in the form of reflection the phenomenon called the mind. Seeing only the reflection the *ajnani* is deluded into the belief that he is a finite being, the *jiva*. If the mind is introverted, through Self-enquiry, into the source of *Aham Vritti*, the 'I-thought', *vasanas* become extinct and in the absence of the reflecting medium, the phenomenon of reflection, namely the mind, disappears, being absorbed into the light of the one Reality, the Heart",[9] incidentally, it may be mentioned that this is why the *jiva* or the individual self is called the reflected Consciousness (*chidabhasa*).

---

7 *Talks with Sri Ramana Maharshi*, T. 28.

8 *Ibid.*, T. 616

9 *Maharshi's Gospel*, Vol.II, last chap.

Viveka Chudamani verse 276 says that *vasanas get extinct to the extent to which the mind is absorbed in the Heart.*

"Contemplation of one's own Self uninterrupted by ideas of external objects is necessary and thereby the instinctive tendencies of the mind which are the causes of birth and death are put down. Until the sole idea of the Self naturally and without effort flows in a continuous current, contemplation should be practised. Then the *vasanas* perish. All the Upanishads direct a man to kill *vasanas* by contemplation of the Self."

Mandukya Upanishad directs the fixing of the mind on the *ardhamatra* or the last syllable of the mental articulation of the sound in 'OM' and remaining thought-free which is virtually fixing the mind on the Heart.

The *Bhagavad Gita* VI. 25-26 says, "With resolute will, gradually get the mind fixed on the Self and obtain mental stillness; thereafter remain thought-free. Whenever the mind gets outward, bring it back and establish it on the Self."

Bhagavan Sri Ramana instructing Kavyakantha Ganapathi Muni on *tapas* said, "If, when a *mantra* is repeated, one keenly watches wherefrom the *mantra* sound emanates, the mind will get absorbed there. That is *Tapas*."

Sri Bhagavan in "*Who am I?*" says, "To keep the mind turned within and abide in the Self is *Atma Vichara*."

Again in *Upadesa Sara* Verse 10 says, "To abide at the source of the ego, that is, the Heart, is *Karma, Bhakthi, Yoga* and *Jnana*." *Abiding in the Heart means to keep the mind focused on the Heart and remaining thought-free.*

Here it should be stated that Heart, *Atman, Brahman*, Self, Spirit, Guru and Void are synonymous. So also *Jiva*, mind, ego, *chidabhasa*, and reflected consciousness are synonymous.

Just as the ether in a pot is no other than the all-pervading ether, the Self in the heart of every individual is no other than the all-pervading Supreme Spirit or God.

10. LOCUS OF THE SELF

"The Self, smaller than the smallest and bigger than the biggest and is hidden in the recess of the heart of living beings" (*Sv. Up.*).

"The Inner Self as big as each one's thumb resides in the heart of everyone" (*Katha valli*).

"The heart is like a lotus inverted. There is a bright spot, atom-like, like the end of a grain of paddy. That spot is like a flame and its crest is the seat of the Self" (*Purusha Suktha*).

"Two digits to the right of the centre of the chest is the Heart like a lotus bud. All the *nadis* emanate from here. Breath, mind and the light of Consciousness originate from here" (Verses 18-19. Sup. to *Truth Revealed*).

11. TO LOCATE THE HEART FOR MEDITATION

Since the breath originates from the heart, to locate the heart for the *sadhana*, watch, with closed eyes, the movement of the breath for a few seconds and observe where breath rises and sinks inside the chest. This is the Heart and should be held as the seat for meditation.

Some people keep the *Sahasrara* (cranium) and some the *Ajna* (the space between the eyebrows) as the seat for meditation; but Sri Bhagavan advocates the Heart only, *as the fixing of the mind only on the Heart results in the extinction of the vasanas and of the mind, whereas it is not so in the case of other centres.*[10]

12. CONCENTRATION

The mind by nature is wandering, propelled by the innate *vasanas*. How to keep the mind concentrated on the Heart is the crux of the *sadhana*. From the ancient days, breath control is advocated. Sri Bhagavan says in *Upadesa Sara* that since the source of breath and mind is the same, if the breath is controlled, mind is automatically controlled; and during the breath restraint if the mind is fixed on the Heart, mind gradually gets defunct. So long as the mind is turned towards and fixed in the Heart, mind is non-receptive to *vasanas* which in turn weaken.

---

[10] *Talks with Sri Ramana Maharshi*, T. 616

Discussing Sage Patanjali's Raja Yoga about the subjugation of the mind, Sri Bhagavan says that '*chitta vritti nirodha*' (control of the activities of the mind) is brought about in sleep, swoon or by starvation; but with the withdrawal of the cause of such torpor, mind gets active again; but in *Maha Yoga*, the practice consists in the withdrawal of the mind into the Self. [11]

13. BREATH CONTROL

For purposes of concentration, *pranayama* is suggested to be practised in the various *yoga sastras*. Bhagavan Sri Ramana says *pranayama* in its entirety is not necessary. Referring to breath control as an aid for concentration he said, "*Bahih pranayama* (external control of breath) is for one not endowed with strength to control the mind. There is no way so sure as that of a sage's company. The external practice must be resorted to by the wise man, if he does not enjoy a sage's company. If in a sage's company, the sage provides the needed strength though unseen by others. If engaged in *japa, dhyana, bhakthi,* etc., just a little control of breath will suffice to control the mind."[12]

Concentration of mind on the Heart destroys *vasanas* and makes the mind pure. Pure mind or *suddha manas* in vedantic parlance is mind free from thoughts. (Thoughts may be pure or impure).

---

[11] *Talks with Sri Ramana Maharshi*, T. 485

[12] *Ibid.*, T. 54

14. PRACTICE

When one tries to calm the mind and starts to meditate, waves of thoughts each in ever more demanding form rush to occupy the cleared field. Without entertaining any of them, as each thought arises, one has to put the question, "To whom is this thought come?". The answer will be "To me." Then put the question "Who am I?" and with the mental articulation of it one must dive into the Heart in search of the source of the "I thought" (vide Step 4.). Such frequent divings into the Heart destroy the particular thought. Treat every successive thought in the same manner. After a little while, you will find you are getting mastery over these thoughts. A particular place and time for *sadhana* are always helpful since by getting into the habit of sitting at a particular place and time, the mind involuntarily starts meditating.

15. DIVING INTO THE HEART

Verse 28, *Truth Revealed*, says:— Just as a diver dives into a well to search for something dropped in it, so must you with restraint of speech and breath dive deep within yourself to find wherefrom the ego rises.

Restraint of speech is advocated in this; but for ordinary aspirants in the initial stages *japa* of 'Who am I' while diving seems to be necessary to prevent the mind from wandering; it may not be so essential for advanced souls who can easily concentrate.

Here the mind while engaged in the search for the source of the ego is given continuous work in the region of the Heart so that the mind is fully concentrated on it and is unable to wander, resulting in the achievement of the aim, *i.e.* the fixity of the mind in the Heart.

In Chapter I, *Maharshi's Gospel* Vol. II, he says "Self-enquiry is not an empty formula. It is more than the repetition of any *mantra*. If the enquiry 'Who am I?' were a mere mental questioning, it would not be of much value. THE VERY PURPOSE OF SELF-ENQUIRY IS TO FOCUS THE ENTIRE MIND AT ITS SOURCE. It is not therefore, a case of one 'I' searching for another 'I'.

"Much less is it an empty formula, for it involves an intense activity of the entire mind to keep it steadily fixed in pure Self-awareness.

"Self-enquiry is the only infallible means, the only direct one to realise the unconditioned absolute Being that you really are."

Just as a person by frequent immersion in water is rid of the dirt of his body, similarly mind, by its frequent immersion in the Heart in a thought-free state, sheds all its accretions and *vasanas* acquired in several births.

On one occasion Sri Bhagavan said, "One requires a form to contemplate; but it is not enough, for can anyone keep looking at an image always? So the image should be complemented by *japa* which helps to fix the mind on the image, in addition to the eyesight. The result of these efforts is concentration of mind, which ends in the goal."[13]

In Maha Yoga, *sadhana* involves search only for the source of the ego; thus an image or object of concept is obviated, as such objects are a source of hindrance to achievement.

Whereas in other yogas, it is considered necessary to cultivate and acquire certain spiritual excellences, as *Sadhana Chathushtaya,* etc., as prerequisites, in Maha Yoga the *sadhana* itself, in its course, confers these excellences without having to cultivate them.[14]

Further in Maha Yoga PRACTICE UNFOLDS THEORY, whereas in other yogas, theory guides practice.

A *sadhaka*, during practice, is impelled to investigate how and when thoughts arise in spite of his resoluteness to prevent them by fixing his mind on the Heart. In the early stages of *sadhana* it is found that the *vasanas* keep besieging the mind all the time. When the mind even for a split-second loses hold of the Heart, the *vasanas* drive a wedge, cause the mind to function, *i.e.,* formulate thoughts and pass them on to the brain which develops them and passes them on to the sense organs, thus concretising thought forms into gross objects. But during breath restraint, the thought the mind was engaged in at the beginning of the restraint, continues to have the hold during the period of restraint, not admitting of intrusion by any other thought.

[13] *Talks with Sri Ramana Maharshi,* T. 401

[14] *Day by Day with Bhagavan,* Vol.I, p. 70.

Hence the concentration. So if the *sadhaka* is careful at the beginning of the restraint of breath to fix the mind on the Heart and practises Self-enquiry and later stillness of mind, he can continue to do so during the full period of restraint.

It should be clearly understood that concentration cannot be had in a few months or years. The way is long and he is a hero who, undaunted by failures, resolutely practises till he achieves the goal. Once concentration is mastered, the rest is easy. Mind unimpeded by *vasanas* strengthens its hold on the Heart.

Guru's Grace is necessary for progress at each step. Frequent prayer to the Guru (Self) for the success of each step and for the removal of mental impediments is very necessary.

After a few years of practice your mind, by such *sadhana*, having got pure, is readily able to absorb all scriptural statements without any reasoning or doubt. Sometimes the knowledge contained therein has already been experienced by you and serves only to verify your experience. A spirit of involuntary surrender sets in. You begin to feel that nothing in the worldly plane is in your hands and that everything is preordained and that you are only like a dry leaf blown about by the winds. Material loss or gain ceases to affect you. Even in your *sadhana* you feel you cannot progress except by Guru's Grace and Grace is had by the amount of effort put in and the effort is not forthcoming unless there is the Guru's Grace — a strange paradox.

Also you would have found that the *sadhana* has resulted in the elimination of the onrush of minor passing thoughts which in the early stages were discouraging you. There is also a natural disinclination to entertain any thoughts. You also try to avoid company and argument as they result in creating *vasanas* which impede your concentration during practice.

You also unconsciously shed all unethical inclinations and weaknesses and acquire spiritual excellences without having to cultivate them because of your habitual rejection of thoughts not relating to the Self.

16. GAPS BETWEEN THOUGHTS

Another noticeable feature is that your mind is getting attenuated. Let us suppose that in a minute six thoughts occurred with split-second intervals between every two of them. This split-second gap between two thoughts is a period of no thoughts, *i.e.*, your natural primal state. *Tripura Rahasya* says when the mind does not create pictures due to absence of thoughts, it is the unmodified state which is its primal and pure condition.

Again in Ch. XVI. *ibid*, it is stated, "Every instant free from thoughts or musings in the wakeful state is the condition of *Samadhi. Samadhi* is simply absence of thoughts."

With the progress of *Sadhana* the gap of no thoughts variously termed as *Sunya*, void or blankness keeps on increasing. In the beginning it is very noticeably felt. Just as a busy housewife confronted with no work looks around and says 'What shall I do next?' similarly mind, accustomed to unceasing thinking, when subject to these gaps involuntarily, expresses itself in words, 'What shall I think about now?'. One has to experience this to believe it.

During the advanced stages of the practice of Step 4 described in the next chapter, which correspond to '*Tanumanasi*', the third *bhumika* of *Jnana Yoga* previously detailed, it is marvellous to find how the mind effortlessly becomes subject to dissection.

Just as a piece of cloth frequently exposed to burning fire loses its strength though retaining its texture, mind, by its constant exposure to the Light of Consciousness, loses its capacity to formulate thoughts; and not only that, the mind declines to think and offers resistance to serious thoughts. At this stage doubts assail you as to whether you are getting into some sort of mental lapse, due to non-convergence of thoughts. This is not a state to be afraid of at all, as the aim of the *sadhana* is the annihilation of the mind.

A state of mental void often involuntarily sets in. Previously the quest for the source of the ego was possible with the full strength of the mind; but now with the mind rarefied as a result of the *sadhana*, diving in the Heart becomes hard and the mind sometimes stands stock still and you automatically keep quiet with the mind simply focused on the Heart. This is how you are thrown into the next step of 'being still'. Sri Bhagavan says *"Upasana* and *dhyana* are possible so long as there is the mind and they must cease with the cessation of the mind. They are mere preliminaries to final eradication of thoughts and the stillness of mind."[15]

17. VASANAS AND SEX

Reverting to *vasanas* it is necessary to be outspoken and not feel delicate about the *vasana* of sex as this was frequently raised even by *sannyasins* before Sri Bhagavan. This *vasana* of sex was acquired and developed in successive births so that it has become an instinct. It is further developed by more enjoyments and by thinking over them. This *vasana* is a frailty common to all, except in rare cases, where it has been weakened by meditation in the previous birth. Aspirants in the spiritual path are much discouraged by these *vasanas*. Indeed, they doubt if it would at all be possible to overcome them. One school of thought believes in sublimating this *vasana* by unremitting devotion to God and rejecting these thoughts as they occur; but most people generally succumb to the weakness and are still faced with the difficulty.

In Ch. XIV of *Self Realisation* a devotee asks Sri Bhagavan:-

There are innumerable *purva* (ancient) *vasanas*. When will they be wiped out?

B.: The more you withdraw into the Self the more they pale off and finally by themselves fade out completely. With firm determination dive deep into the Self and merge there.

[15] *Talks with Sri Ramana Maharshi*, T. 433.

Vichara must be practised as long as the *vasanas* issue forth to cause thoughts to occur.

On another occasion to a question whether distractions due to previous tendencies could be got rid of, Sri Bhagavan replied with emphasis and with a view to carry conviction, "Yes. Many have done so. Believe it! They did so because they believed they could. *Vasanas* can be obliterated. It is done by concentration on that which is free from *vasanas* and yet their core."[16]

Since this *vasana* is a cumulative one, ancient and deep rooted, it is the last to fade. Maha Yoga when regularly practised gradually weakens this *vasana*. With the practice of the Step 4 detailed in the next chapter and with the gradual attenuation of the mind, the power to bring out this thought decreases and later with more practice of the mind abiding in the Heart these *vasanas* do not trouble you. Of course a frequent prayer to eliminate these *vasanas* and a slight but sincere effort to reject these thoughts or a dive into the Heart as soon as they appear are very helpful.

Wise men liken the *sadhakas* who have not overcome this weakness to filling a leaky vessel with water, for what is acquired by *sadhana* is lost by this weakness.

Prayer when daily offered for spiritual advancement, by itself, becomes *tapas*. The prayer for the eradication of this *vasana* apart from its efficacy in the grant of the boon

---

[16] *Talks with Sri Ramana Maharshi*, T. 28

immediately or later has its psychological effect on the aspirant, particularly when offered earnestly and daily as it creates a good *vasana*.

Earnest spiritual aspirants if they do not attain their goal in the current birth continue to be spiritual aspirants in the next birth also and the *samskaras* created now by practice and prayer are carried over as good and substantial assets to the next birth when they will easily find expression in surroundings congenial for the fulfilment of their aspiration.

Incidentally it may be mentioned that great geniuses, political, spiritual, scientific and of other arts are not due to accidents of birth but due to the cumulative effect of their sustained effort, research, practice, and reflection in their respective fields in their previous births, finding culmination in the current life.

One visitor queried if the *vasanas* could not be got rid of if the senses are surfeited to satiation point. Sri Bhagavan replied that such indulgence will be like pouring petrol to put out burning fire.

When celibacy was mooted, Sri Bhagavan brushed it aside and said that it was one among the many aids to realisation and did not insist on it, meaning that the craving will wear off with the practice of the Yoga.

18. STILLNESS OF MIND

With the attenuation of the mind, stillness of mind should be practised. Sri Bhagavan says stillness is the sole requisite for realisation.[17]

In Buddhism also stillness is variously emphasised for the attainment of Buddhahood.

Sri Bhagavan used frequently to quote the Biblical maxim "Be still and know that I am God."

His own parallel quotations are:- "If you are free from thoughts and yet aware, you are That Perfect Being."[18]

"When free from thoughts, you are infinite intelligence, the Self."[19]

"Thought-free mind merged in the heart is *Chit* itself."[20]

"All that is required to realise the Self is 'to be still'."[21]

"Atma is realised by *mruta manas*, that is, mind devoid of thoughts and turned inward."[22]

So stillness of mind and the consequent virtual extinction of the mind are necessary for Self-realisation.

Advaita Bodha Deepika says, "It is not difficult to kill the mind. Though for the ignorant it may be difficult, for the discerning few it is very easy. Never think of anything but

---

17 *Talks with Sri Ramana Maharshi*, T. 338.

18 *Ibid.*, T. 609.

19 *Ibid.*, T. 609.

20 *Ibid.*, T. 480.

21 *Ibid.*, T. 589.

22 *Ibid.*, T. 379.

the unbroken Self. By a long practice of this you will easily forget the non-self. It cannot be hard to remain still without thinking anything. Let no thoughts rise in the mind; always think of the Self. In this way all worldly thoughts will vanish and thought of the Self alone will remain. When this gets steady, forget even this and without thinking 'I am the Self' remain as the Self. By this practice your mind will be extinct and you will forget all and remain as the Self."[23]

It is not desirable for an aspirant to start practising stillness of the mind from the very beginning itself instead of the practice of "Who am I?" because of the rush of thoughts. Unless the mind is at least to some extent attenuated by the practice of "Who am I?", the attempt at stillness of mind may take a longer time or may end in frustration. Of course this is not intended for *sadhakas* who have attained already a certain amount of attenuation of mind.

While Sri Bhagavan was discoursing on the stillness of mind a cultured lady visitor asked, "What should be done to remain free from thoughts as advised by you? Is it only the enquiry of 'Who am I'?"

B: Only to remain still. Do it and see.

The lady: It is impossible.

B: Exactly. For the same reason the enquiry 'Who am I?' is advised.[24]

Stillness of mind or Silence can also be got by keeping the mind empty, watchfully dispelling thoughts,

---

[23] *Advaita Bodha Deepika*, p. 117.

[24] *Talks with Sri Ramana Maharshi*, T. 322.

having emptiness of mind as the sole aim, without the contemplation of the Self as the background. Trance resulting from such emptiness can give some sort of pleasure due to the absence of thoughts; but this alone will not do; and it sometimes ends disastrously. It does not lead to liberation. This method should be guarded against.

This warning is intended only for those wanting to find and pursue a shortcut in their *sadhana*. Stillness or emptiness of mind or voidness arising from the partial eradication of the *vasanas* as a result of contemplation of the Self is what should be aimed at. This voidness is a state of intense concentration. In the early stages even a pin-drop noise causes bodily shock which shatters you to pieces. Besides this, stillness or the thought-free natural state also scorches the *vasanas*. Sri Bhagavan says the *vasanas* will "be scorched if only you remain as you truly are," meaning in your primal pure state.[25]

It will be noticed that the mental articulation of "Who am I?" is in the initial stages used for the rejection of thoughts and in the next stage "Who am I?", meaning "What is the source of the 'I thought'?" is used for training the mind to dive into the Heart, resulting in the gradual attenuation of the mind and the elimination of *vasanas* due to the exposure of the mind to the light of consciousness while diving. Thereafter stillness of mind is obtained when the mind is engaged in focusing on the Heart without any mental articulation.

---

[25] *Talks with Sri Ramana Maharshi*, T. 219.

19. THE INNER VOICE

The Inner Voice is heard as you hear your own mental articulation. It is mostly heard when in a state bordering on trance. There is no mistaking it. If you happen to be one of those used to early morning meditation at 2 or 3 a.m. and if by chance you oversleep, it rouses you up calling you by your name. In the beginning, when not used to it, you wonder wherefrom externally the voice comes. Later you understand it. Sometimes the Inner Voice says "Still sleeping?"; or if by inadvertance, you have taken *tamasic* food overnight resulting in your inability to meditate and feeling inclined to sleep, it chides you; but if by over-meditating in the previous night or any other reasonable cause you feel sleepy and unable to meditate and feel acutely remorseful for losing the period, it says "Don't worry". How at every step it handles you more than a fond mother!

When meditation tapers off to stillness or trance the Inner Voice, the voice of the Self or Guru, is heard from within to clear whatever doubts you may be labouring under. At times it quells your meditation and comes like a flash and has its say. A wise *sadhaka* should at once jot down such instructions for sometimes it is difficult to comprehend their meaning all at once, in some cases the expressions are so classical that you have to refer to the dictionary for most words: besides they are cryptic and meaningful and the language is inimitably beautiful, particularly in the case of

Sri Bhagavan's devotees. If you fail to jot them down, then and there, you cannot recall them.

In this connection one is aptly reminded of Sri Bhagavan's quotations from Sage Thayumanavar, "Oh, Lord! Coming with me all along the several births, never abandoning me and finally rescuing me!"[26] and again from the author of *Kaivalya Navaneetham,* "Oh Guru! You have always been with me, watching me through several births and ordaining my course."[27] Unless Sri Bhagavan had himself this experience he would not have referred to others' experience about it. This also explains Sri Bhagavan's instructions to the American gentleman at the time of his parting: "The Inner Guru is never silent."[28]

Mahatma Gandhi relied very much on the Inner Voice which guided him throughout in planning his political movement. Can a movement guided by God fail?

Sri Bhagavan was a regular reader of Gandhi's weekly *Harijan* and occasionally got Gandhi's experiences in *Harijan* read out in the hall.

20. SAMADHI

Real *Atma Vichara* begins only when one is off the mental waves and abides in the Heart. By unswerving constancy in the Self, like the ceaseless unbroken filamentary

---

[26] *Talks with Sri Ramana Maharshi*, T. 398.
[27] *Ibid.*, 425.
[28] *Ibid.*, T. 508.

flow of oil, is generated the *Nirvikalpa Samadhi*.[29] Every Yogi's aim is to achieve the *Nirvikalpa Samadhi* for its beneficial spiritual effects.

Samadhi is a sort of trance. Sri Rama in *Rama Gita* tells Hanuman there are over a hundred *samadhis*. There are the *Hatha Yoga* and *Raja Yoga samadhis*. They are all treated in their respective treatises. But in Maha Yoga the *samadhis* an aspirant meets with during the course of the *sadhana* are 1. *Kevala Nirvikalpa Samadhi*, 2. *Savikalpa Samadhi*, 3. *Nirvikalpa Samadhi* and 4. *Sahaja Samadhi*.

Kevala Nirvikalpa Samadhi is experienced during *Tanumanasi* or the advanced stages of Step 4. In *Kevala Nirvikalpa Samadhi* the mind is immersed in the Light of Consciousness for a short while and is pulled back by the *vasanas* that have not been destroyed. In this state, awareness with calmness of mind is experienced.

Mind holding on to the Self with effort is *Savikalpa Samadhi*. In other words when the mind is fixed on the object of meditation for a particular length of time unobstructed by the least ripple of thought it is *Savikalpa Samadhi*. *Savikalpa* means with differentiation of subject and object *i.e.*, the meditator and the object of meditation.

Constant practice of *Savikalpa Samadhi* leads to *Nirvikalpa Samadhi*. Mind merged in Reality and remaining unaware of the world is *Nirvikalpa Samadhi*. In this state the subject and object, *i.e.*, the meditator and the meditated, fuse

---

[29] *Talks with Sri Ramana Maharshi*, T. 349.

into a mass of consciousness. On coming out of this *samadhi* the meditator recalls the *samadhi* experience and remembering what he has read in the scriptures to be identical with his experience he realises himself as 'I am That'. This recollection of the *samadhi* experience and his identification as 'I am That' is called *Pratyabhijna Jnana*. It is only this *Pratyabhijna Jnana* that completely destroys ignorance *i.e.*, duality. This is fully explained in Chap. XVII. *Tripura Rahasya*.

21. EFFECTS OF NIRVIKALPA SAMADHI

Viveka Chudamani says, "When the mind is purified by *sadhana*, one passes from *Savikalpa* to *Nirvikalpa Samadhi* and thereafter directly to Self-realisation. This *Nirvikalpa Samadhi* results in the severance of *Chit-Jada-Granthi*, destruction of all *vasanas* and the cognisance of all manifestations as the Self without effort. The difference of you, I, this, that, etc., disappears."

Sri Bhagavan says that it is only up to the attainment of *Nirvikalpa Samadhi* that effort is necessary:- "Then the Beyond takes hold of you. Your effort cannot reach there. With Self-realisation only, real and incessant *tapas* results."[30] This *tapas* is effortless. Just as a trajectile to reach the moon is powered to overcome the earth's gravitation initially and to overcome the space of weightlessness till it is thrown into the field of the moon's attraction, when the moon's attraction alone prevails and gathers the

[30] *Talks with Sri Ramana Maharshi*, T. 57.

trajectile to the moon, similarly the aspirant by his effort overcomes the *vasanas* and the mind, which prevent his abiding in the Self. After a period of mindlessness and *Nirvikalpa Samadhi* he is attracted and forcibly held by the Self till he is transformed into the Self. After *Nirvikalpa Samadhi* he becomes a *Jivanmukta, i.e.*, liberated even when alive. Thereafter there is no effort on his part. He is only passive to the influence of the Self which effects the transformation. Just like the steel stuck to a magnet, the mind is held and overpowered by the Self and is released only after it is completely transformed.

Sri Ramakrishna while so overpowered by the Self was unconscious of the body and its needs had to be tended to and the saint fed by his nephew Hriday.

Bhagavan Sri Ramana after his arrival at Tiruvannamalai was in a similar condition for several weeks. The grip of the Self on him was so great and persistent that he was absolutely unconscious of the passing of the days and nights and of his body and its needs and he had to be forcibly fed.

In the tenth verse of *The Ten Verses on Arunachala,* recalling his experience he says, "I have discovered a new thing. This Hill, the Lodestone of lives, arrests the movements of anyone who so much as thinks of It, draws him face to face with It, and fixes him motionless like itself, to feed upon his soul thus ripened. What a wonder is this! O souls, beware of It and live! Such a destroyer of lives is this magnificent Arunachala, which shines within the Heart!"

22. EXPERIENCE OF SELF-REALISATION

Talking about the experience at the time of Realisation Sri Bhagavan said, "Realisation is called *Vritti Jnana*. You can feel yourself one with the One that exists; the whole body becomes a mere power, a force current; your life becomes a needle drawn to a huge mass of magnet and as you go deeper and deeper you become a mere centre and not even that, for you become mere consciouness. There are no thoughts and cares any longer; they are shattered at the threshold; it is an inundation; you are a mere straw; you are swallowed alive; but it is very delightful, for you become the very thing that swallows you. This is the union of *jiva* with *Brahman*, the loss of ego in the real Self, the destruction of ignorance, the attainment of truth."[31]

Speaking about this on another occasion he said, "After tasting such bliss even once, one will repeatedly try to regain it. Having experienced the bliss of peace once, no one would like to be out of it or engage himself otherwise."

After gaining *samadhi*, it is stated, *samadhi* must be continuously practised till *Sahaja Samadhi* results. Even after gaining *samadhi*, the experience of *jnana* is spasmodic on account of the *vasanas* not having been completely destroyed. For *jnana* to get *dridha* (firm) one must have recourse to the rememberance of "I am not the body" and to recall the *samadhi* experience. These eradicate the *vasanas*. Then dawns

[31] *Sat Darsana Bhashya*, XXXII.

the *Sahaja* state. One who remains in the primal sahaja state of BE-ing, that is, free from thoughts without effort, unaffected by internals or externals, *i.e.*, not reacting to them, is said to be in *SAHAJA SAMADHI*. He who is fixed in this pristine *sahaja* state is in automatic and incessant *tapas*. This pristine nature of the Self is effortless and spontaneous *tapas*. Engaged in such incessant *tapas*, ONE DEVELOPS MOMENT AFTER MOMENT, on the spiritual plane. This incessant *tapas* leads to the manifestation of all powers. If one's *prarabdha* is that way he may even develop thaumaturgic powers. There is no difference between a *Jnani* and a *Siddha* even in granting boons including *Atma Labha* (Self-realisation). The last stanza of *Sri Ramana Gita* Chap. XVIII reads : "The glory of *Siddhas* is beyond imagination; they are equal to Siva Himself in being able to grant boons." All this is explained in Chap. XI *Sri Ramana Gita*, and after serial 57 of *Talks with Sri Ramana Maharshi*.

The *Muktikopanishad* says, "When the mind does not think at all, being completely devoid of *vasanas*, then dawns the state of mindlessness, which confers the great peace."

The question may arise as to how anyone could function at all without mind. Just as a pot filled with grains and emptied of its contents is filled with *akasa* (ether) which was all along there, similarly mind emptied of thoughts (what is left over) is *Chit* itself which is infinite knowledge.

With the destruction of mind, *Kartritwa* (I-am-the-doer idea) vanishes. Every word uttered and every action done is God's.

In this connection it will be interesting to recall what Sri Ramakrishna expressed once : "Just like a grain dealer with a heap of grains pushes them gradually towards the man who measures them out, I felt someone behind me supplying me with a torrent of ideas to be given out."

To a question by a lawyer devotee if the day-long examination of him at the commission of enquiry about Asramam affairs caused Bhagavan Sri Ramana much strain, he replied, "I did not use my mind and so there was no strain. Let them examine me for a thousand days : I don't mind."[32] The inference is obvious.

While the mental articulation of "Who am I?" or "Be still" is useful in the initial stages, effort must be made to give it up totally, as such articulation stands in the way of concentration and stillness of mind. Similarly, breath restraint should be given up when one feels one could concentrate without this aid. Of course, one can have recourse to them again whenever the mind is much agitated and is uncontrollable for any reason.

While regular and fixed hours of practice are for novices, earnest aspirants burdened by no activities must use all available time for practice. They must keep on increasing their period of practice to about ten hours or more. This increase must be gradual and not steep. The author was mostly using the morning hours of 2 to 6, 8 to 11 a.m. 2 to 3, 4 to 6 and 8 to 9 p.m. and that too in his 66th

[32] *Talks with Sri Ramana Maharshi*, T. 281.

year onwards. Initially, it would be hard to meditate for such long periods; but if there is earnestness, the difficulty would not be felt. Then there is the Guru's Grace aiding and encouraging you. As the early morning meditation is most important, the aspirant should be regular in practice then. It would be hard to keep awake at that time and harder still to meditate. The author in trying to overcome this sleep had recourse to various devices, but later found a decoction of equal quantities of tea and dried mint with milk effective. A little quantity of it in the flask, using a couple of sips whenever yawning started, warded off sleep. While pure tea by itself prevented sleep, it caused waves after waves of thoughts to rise and prevent meditation; but a mixture of tea and mint, while it kept one awake, overcame the turbulent action of the mind and lulled it, making it easy to meditate.

While not meditating, the mind should be kept engaged in reading *Sri Ramana Gita, Who am I, Self-enquiry, Vivekachudamani* and other books bearing on this *sadhana*. At other times, one should engage himself in the repetition of the *Japa* of "Who am I?".

The *Japa* of 'Who am I?' in the beginning may appear ludicrous for those used to 'Siva', 'Rama', 'Krishna', etc.; but it must be understood that this *japa* of 'Who am I?' makes one involuntarily fix the mind on the Heart, which is the aim of the *sadhana*. Besides Sri Bhagavan says, 'Who am I?' is the best of all *japas*.[33]

---

[33] *Talks with Sri Ramana Maharshi*, T. 72.

When well advanced in the practice of Step 4, say after five years, the aspirant should try to practise with eyes open occasionally, as it helps one to meditate while walking or sitting idle. This may also be attempted while lying on the left.

The following passage culled from the introduction to his Tamil translation *Vivekachudamani* by Sri Bhagavan will be found to be of great significance to earnest *sadhakas* in the very late stages, say, after ten years or more of practice of Step 4 and when they have been able to meditate with eyes open.

"Like butter being forced out of the curd by ceaseless churning, the mind, used as a churn-staff, should be fixed on the Heart and the latter ceaselessly churned. This unswerving and unremitting churning, like the continuous flow of filamentary oil, automatically results in *Sahaja Nirvikalpa Samadhi*."

The above passage in one's own language must be frequently repeated mentally and every word of this must be ruminated upon and well understood. The frequent repetition of this passage enthuses and stimulates the aspirant to practical effort in that direction.

"Just as a red-hot iron ball can behave as fire, so also the mind suffused with Self-enquiry is not different from the Self."[34]

The aspirants should not allow the mind even for a moment to slip into materialistic or sensual fields.

---

[34] *Sri Ramana Gita*, IX. 19.

Vivekachudamani says such slipping even for a split-second hurls the *sadhaka* headlong into a materialistic abyss; he has to put in a deal of time and practice to regain the previously attained stage. Frequent prayer to the Self to prevent this relapse brings about the desired effect.

Vasanas acquired and accumulated in several births can only be eradicated by long continued meditation over a period of some decades depending on the period of steady fixity of the mind on the Heart. Though in the beginning the *sadhaka* is impatient for results, later, he is more intent on the *sadhana* than on its fruits.

Nor need one feel discouraged that one's efforts and *sadhana* for Self-realisation will be wasted if the goal is not reached in the current life.

Sage Vidyaranya says, "When meditation has not got mature in this life, it will become so at death or in the world of *Brahman*, where getting a direct knowledge of *Brahman*, he gets emancipation". (*Panchadasi*, IX. 136.)

In *Bhagavad Gita* Ch. VI. 40-46 Lord Krishna, in reply to Arjuna, stated that those performing such *sadhanas*, if they die before achieving their aim, are reborn in highly spiritually minded families and, starting from where they left off in their previous birth, complete their *sadhana*.

To a similar question by Sri Rama as to what will be the fate of one who dies having reached the first, second or third *bhumikas*, Sage Vasishta said:

"Should one satisfy the qualifications required of him in the three *jnana* states then all his *karmas* will cease to exist. Then *Devas* will conduct him in their divine vehicle to *Devaloka* and other places where he will feast his eyes on the pleasant sceneries of Meru, Elysian gardens and beautiful damsels. With the expiry of the enjoyment all the two-fold *karmas* will perish completely and then he will descend on earth as a *jnani*. He will incarnate in a family of the wise replete with enormous wealth, good qualities and purity of mind and body and will unerringly follow the path of *jnana* since he had already subjected himself to a rigorous course of discipline."

Once an individual has got into the first *bhumika* of *jnana yoga*, he will be made to obtain liberation whether he likes it or not; because it was not the individual's will or effort that made him take up this *yoga* but the sustained motiveless actions dedicated to God in several previous births that forced him to this *yoga*. Just as a man with a ticket for Delhi in the Delhi Mail is taken to the destination whatever may happen to the mail or the rails, so can a man be assured of final liberation once he has got into the first *bhumika* of *jnana yoga*.

For those *jnana yogis* whose aim is only liberation from *samsara* and who are not keen on Self-Realisation there is the other easy way of escape by meditation on the Heart at the time of death. Force of habit of rejection of mundane thoughts and the force of habit of easily getting into meditation on the Lord in the recess of their Heart makes it easy for these *yogis* to meditate on Him even at the time of death.

In *Srimad Bhagavatham* Ch. XII. Bk. 3. 49 Sage Suka tells King Parikshit, "With all your being meditate on Him in your heart with a concentrated mind while dying, you will thereby attain the supreme goal. Those mediating on Him while dying, He leads them to the oneness with Him."

At no stage of the *sadhana* should pace be forced but must be gradual. Nor should one get impatient with one's progress. Sri Bhagavan used to express that the fact that one is persisting in the *sadhana* is itself an indication of progress and Guru's Grace.

If the practice is perfect at any stage, it will be overlapping the next so that the *sadhaka* is automatically thrown into the next. Let it be understood that Guru's Grace is absolutely necessary for one's progress and if the *sadhaka* is regular and earnest in practice he is not forsaken but encouraged in several subtle ways, perceptible and intelligible.

Questioned about the bestowal of such Divine Grace on a *sadhaka* Sri Bhagavan, suffused with a divine light in his face, declared in unequivocal language : "Divine Grace is essential for Realisation. It leads one to God-realisation. BUT SUCH GRACE IS VOUCHSAFED ONLY TO HIM WHO IS A TRUE DEVOTEE OR A YOGIN, WHO HAS STRIVEN HARD AND CEASELESSLY ON THE PATH TOWARDS FREEDOM."[35]

One need not feel discouraged by middle or advanced age to begin this *sadhana* of Maha Yoga. Sri Bhagavan has

---

[35] *Talks with Sri Ramana Maharshi*, T. 29.

often expressed that age is no bar for this *sadhana*, whereas age restriction is indicated for Raja Yoga.

Those that have taken to this Maha Yoga must from the beginning try to wean the mind away from the worship of external gods like the images of various Hindu gods and transfer such worship to the Self within. In the beginning, it may be a little hard but with practice and Guru's Grace you gradually get used to look upon the Self as the Supreme God. Worship and prayer to the Self is more efficacious than to an image.

Also as you advance in this Maha Yoga you begin to feel and realise that all rituals and ceremonies are comparatively of less value and that time spent in these is better utilised in *Atma Vichara*.

23. TATTWA JNANA

From the beginning of the *sadhana*, simultaneously with the practice of Self enquiry, the *bhavana* (the mental visualisation) of : "The whole manifestation including the world is *Atman*. That *Atman* alone am I," should be daily practised, as ultimately after realisation one sees all objects are superimpositions on the substratum, the *Atman*. Sage Vasishta instructing Sri Rama in *Yoga Vasishta*, and Sri Rama instructing Hanuman in *Muktikopanishad* say : " The practices of *Tattwa jnana*, of the extinction of the *vasanas* and of the mind, should all three be simultaneous. They should not be taken up at different periods and done separately."

The practice of the above *bhavana* has another beneficial effect. The *sastras* say and Bhagavan has also said, "The practice of the *bhavana* of 'I am the Self ' is the highest virtue. Even a moment's *dhyana* to that effect is enough to destroy all the *sanchita karma*. It works like the sun before whom darkness is dispelled. If one remains always in such *dhyana*, can any sin, however heinous it may be, survive this *dhyana*?"[36]

The *smritis* state that even a moment's *Atma Vichara* has the effect of bathing in all the sacred rivers, of the merit of the performance of a thousand *yagas* and of having liberated one's ancestors from births.

For one practising Maha Yoga even *prarabdha* is much mitigated in its effects and the individual does not feel it much, though to the onlooker it may appear that he is suffering.

Sri Krishna extolling the path of *Jnana* to Arjuna in the *Bhagavad Gita* Ch. IV. 35-37 says, "Of all the sinners, if you happen to be the worst, get over the sins by *Jnana*. Just as a burning fire turns wood to ashes, the fire of *Jnana* reduces all *karma* to ashes."

CONCLUSION

Though a general outline of the scheme of practice of Maha Yoga is given here, the aspirant need not rigidly follow the scheme, for if once he has got well established in the 4th Step, outlined in the next chapter, and has practised it for a decade or more, he will be guided further by the

---

[36] *Talks with Sri Ramana Maharshi*, T. 536.

experience gained and by the Inner Self, the Guru. There need be no doubt about this.

It is amazing how, at the right time, you come across books dealing with the particular aspect of the *sadhanas* you are practising, as if by chance, but really by the grace of the Guru. What hitherto could not be understood, though you might have read it several times previously, becomes transparently clear now without effort.

The steps detailed after Step 4, as also the various *samadhis* indicating the stages in the progress of the path are intended only to serve as landmarks, because you get into the next step automatically. Indeed, if the aspirant strives in the culture of the Inner Self as indicated in Step 4 only and sticks to it, everything else will be automatically added on to him. Sri Bhagavan says, "All you need to do is to find the source of the ego and abide there. Your effort can extend only thus far. Then the Beyond will take care of itself."[37]

What is very necessary in the beginning is faith in the teachings and perseverance in the practice. No appreciable benefit could be experienced for nearly a couple of years initially and one should not give up practice on account of it, for though the progress in the *sadhana* could not be felt by a novice but the effect of the practice is there. No effort or practice in the cultivation of the Inner Self is lost.

External breath restraint is a great potential aid. Indeed, without it, 99.9 per cent of the aspirants cannot progress

---

[37] *Talks with Sri Ramana Maharshi*, T. 197.

appreciably; much less could they understand the teachings of Sri Bhagavan unless they put the teachings in practice and cultivate them for a few years. In fact, 'Dive deep,' 'Merge in the Self,' 'Inhere in the Self,' 'Go to the source of the Ego,' 'Abide in the Self,' 'Remain as the Self,' 'Be Yourself,' etc., will all remain inexplicable and not understandable to novices unless and until one has attained a certain stage and ripeness by practice. Till then they will be mere verbiage. No amount of explanations will clarify them nor need one attempt to understand them but rest content with the feeling that they will get clearer with practice and Guru's grace.

In the later stages of the *sadhana*, the *sadhaka* is often involved involuntarily in introspection which helps him to arrive at a correct estimate of his progress, as he correlates his experience with the teachings. This again infuses confidence and optimism in his *sadhana* for achievement; for the conviction grows in him that even a moment's cultivation of the Self is not lost, just as even a pie put in the bank is added to the bank account.

Sometimes, during the later stages of the *sadhana*, the *sadhaka* gets tired of this mental gymnastics and is inclined to give it up, but the impetus of the previous practice and the grace of the Self push him on. He feels helpless like one caught in the force of a torrential flood. He can neither stop nor retrace but must passively move with the current. Caught in the tiger's jaws, where is the escape?

The feeling grows in him, like that of a child towards its mother, that the Inner Self will look after him and see him through. He is frequently reminded of the sayings in *Kaivalya*, "Oh Guru! You have been always with me watching me and ordaining my course."

Those whose *sadhana* is different from this Maha Yoga need not take to this, for everyone is influenced by his *purva samskaras* (previous tendencies). But Sri Bhagavan has repeatedly expressed that those having recourse to *pranayama* practices can with great advantage use them for *Atma Vichara*.

Chapter II

THE TECHNIQUE OF MAHA YOGA

Rising in the morning at about 4 a.m. have a wash or bath and prostrating before the photo of your Guru or of Bhagavan Sri Ramana Maharshi, pray to him to guide you in meditation.

Step l. Facing north or east sit in a comfortable position and with eyes closed watch the movements of your breath for a few minutes and observe where the breath rises and sinks in the chest inside. This is the HEART and should be held as the seat for meditation.

Step 2. With closed eyes and with *the mental eye or the mind centred in the Heart repeat* 'Who am I?' in your own language without stopping, for at least fifteen minutes, gradually increasing the period to one hour. You must on no account get up till the fixed period is over. See that the *japa* is continuous. Do the same in the evening for the same period.

Step 3. After a few months when well established in the second step, with closed eyes after a quick exhalation restrain the breath outside without inhaling (external *kumbhaka*) as long as possible without strain, repeating 'Who am I?' all the while and inhale. Keep the mental eye fixed on the Heart always. Do this five times in the morning and five times in the evening gradually increasing it to twenty times or more with a minute's rest, *i.e.*, normal breathing after five such *kumbhakas*.

When thoughts interrupt you as they will, do not go away with the thought but immediately put the question "To whom has the thought come?". The answer will be "To me". Then question "Who am I?". Keep on repeating "Who am I?" with the method aforesaid, *i.e.*, with the mind fixed on the Heart and with external *kumbhaka*. Do not be discouraged by the number of thoughts that come, but kill them all as they appear by the above method. In all the practices herein mentioned the vital part of the practice is the fixing of the mind on the Heart which is located as mentioned previously.

You should, after each sitting, try to look back on your meditation to see if thoughts hindered you less or more and try to find the cause of it. In most cases it may be traced to the kind of food taken. Eggs, meat and vegetables like onions, garlic, radish, etc., and sleep-inducing drinks should be avoided totally. Pure cow's milk for the night food is very helpful for night meditation. Doing *japa* of "Who am I?" daily, prior to going to sleep in the bed, makes you do it automatically even while asleep and it is conducive to good meditation in the morning. One desirous of early morning meditation should be satisfied with a half meal for the night.

(Breath restraint or the pause between complete exhalation and inhalation is called 'external *Kumbhaka*').

Step 4. When well established in the last step, try to dive into the Heart during external *kumbhaka* (vide verse 28, 29 *Truth Revealed* and the annotations : Appendix A). Slowly exhale and watch the exhalation movement in the chest. With the sinking movement in the chest dive into the Heart with the mental articulation of "Who am I?". Imagine you are diving into a well to search for something dropped in it. With the breath restrained outside, keep searching for the source of the ego in the Heart with the mental eye just as you would for any small thing in a dark room, feeling for it on the floor with your fingers. Throw out the remaining breath in the lungs and again do the search, all the while repeating "Who am I?" *meaning wherefrom does the 'I' arise*. Ordinarily 20 to 30 seconds of external *kumbhaka* is ample; but those used to *pranayama* can restrain breath longer, but it should be without strain.

You will find this sort of fixing the mind on the Heart with external *kumbhaka* gives you concentration. Any external noise at this juncture in the early stages will cause you sudden bodily shock. This is a proof of your concentration.

This practice after some time may be developed to make the mind do the search without any mental articulation, so that there will be vocal silence and the quest is made with mental *vritti* only.

The fourth step is the essential practice of the Maha Yoga as it eradicates several minor *vasanas* which were initially clamorous and obstructed meditation. It also causes attenuation of the mind. One has to spend several years in the practice of this step to derive its full benefits. Even while practising subsequent steps, when the mind is much agitated for any reason, a few minutes practice of this step will restore tranquillity.

MENTAL STILLNESS

With the progress of the *sadhana,* a time will come when you will find it hard to practise Self-enquiry on account of the mind having got attenuated probably after about ten years or less. It is at this stage you should take to the practice of "stillness of mind".

Step 5. As you throw out the breath simply say once "Be still" and during external *kumbhaka* try to remain thought-free, with the mind fixed on the Heart and avoid any mental articulation during the breath restraint.

Step 6. When sufficiently well established in the previous step *try to remain thought-free normally, i.e.*, without breath restraint and without any mental articulation.

At this stage you have to be careful not to fall asleep, for in the waking state when there are no thoughts you are likely to slip into sleep. Awareness is kept up by the mind being fixed on the Heart. Real *Atma Vichara* begins only here, *i.e.*, when you are fixed on the Heart and are off the mental waves. Remaining in this state results in the extinction of mind and the annihilation of *vasanas*. (Steps 4 to 6 correspond to *Tanumanasi*, the 3rd *bhumika* of *Jnana Yoga*.)

Step 7. When well established in Step 6, cultivate remaining thought-free normally with mind supportless (*niralamba*), *i.e.*, mind not fixed on the Heart nor abiding anywhere whatsoever.

Deep quiescence for a prolonged period eventually results in the experience of Pure Awareness, leading to the goal.

One can distinguish fits of *samadhi* from sleep. In *samadhi* one's head remains erect and one is vaguely aware of external noises. There is also awareness with calmness of mind: not so in the case of sleep.

(N.B.:- The above technique, though graduated, closely follows Sri Bhagavan's teachings, *viz.*, (1) the mind must be fixed in the Heart with *kevala kumbhaka*, and (2) the introverted mind should search for the source of the ego and abide there.)

OM TAT SAT

APPENDIX A

TRUTH REVEALED

by SRI BHAGAVAN

Verses bearing on the practice of the Maha Yoga with a running translation of the annotations as expounded to 'WHO' (Sri K. Lakshmana Sarma) by Sri Bhagavan.

The method indicated hereunder is for the mind to merge itself in the Heart and get itself destroyed. The annihilated state of mind is the state of *Turiya*. The state of *laya* does not lead to *Turiya*. *Laya* is obtained during sleep, stupor or by *hatha yoga* practices. Just as sleep cannot lead to *Turiya*, the other *mano laya* (stupor) practices cannot lead to it. Hence those that obtain *mano laya* will continue to remain as *ajnanis* after waking from that state. IN THE WAKING STATE, MIND INTROVERTING MUST REACH THE SOURCE AND GET MERGED THERE.

Verse 28. "Just as a man would dive in order to get something that had fallen into the water, so one should dive into one's Self with a keen one-pointed mind controlling speech and breath and quest for the place wherefrom the ego rises."

The *sadhana* described here is to introvert and dive deep with a one-pointed mind in search of the source of the ego in the Heart. By the expression 'diving deep' it follows that the heart is the seat of the *Atma* and it is hence inferred that the mind should get introverted in the search for the Self. Introversion means that the mind not being extroverted should be entirely absorbed in the quest. In fact there is no such thing as the Heart being the seat of the *Atma*. HEART IS ATMA itself. The search that is indicated here is the means for the mind IN THE WAKING STATE TO MERGE IN THE ATMA. If during *vichara* one gets sleep, it gets futile, for *Jnana* cannot dawn during sleep.

There is no need for the practice of *pranayama* for the restraint of breath. Sri Bhagavan says that if the entirely absorbed mind with a strong will introverts itself in the search for the Self, the breath will subside by itself.

He used to indicate another method for the subsidence of breath. It is, to breathe naturally and watch the inhalation and the exhalation. If the mind keeps watching the breath movements, the breath will gradually subside by itself.

Like the diver in the water one should dive deep in the Heart with a one-pointed mind and a determined will. Sri Bhagavan further says that the pearl diver dives into the water with a heavy stone tied to him. The *sadhaka* should similarly tie the stone of *vairagya* to him and dive deep into the Heart. One-pointedness and *vairagya* strengthen the mind. In fact both are the same. One with a mind wanderingly inclined is weak and unfit for *vichara* or to realise the Self. One fortified with *vairagya* and with intense desire for realisation of the Self and a determined will is strong.

Self-realisation is not for him who is weak, say the *Upanishads*. Those only can be called strong and courageous who are possessed of *vairagya*, one-pointed mind and armed with strong determination to achieve. For one to realise the Self what else is necessary?

Sri Bhagavan says that if during *sadhana* mind establishes itself steadily, a power from within emerges, takes hold of the mind and gets it united with the Self. The ripe souls yield themselves to this influence without resisting, whereas others extrovert themselves without submitting to its influence. Therefore the mind should be strengthened spiritually by *bhakti*, *vairagya* and *viveka*.

Verse 29. Without even uttering the world 'I', the mind diving deep within and searching for its source is the *sadhana* in *Jnana marga*. The *dhyana* 'I am not this (body)', 'I am That (*Brahman*)', apart from being aids to that *sadhana* cannot be *vichara*.

In some *Vedantic* scriptures the path indicated is different. It is stated therein that realisation is obtained by *Sravana, Manana* and *Nididhyasana*. *Sravana* is the hearing of the meaning of the *Maha vakhyas* from one's Guru. *Manana* is the mental rumination on its meaning and *Nididhyasana* is the incessant contemplation of its meaning. This *dhyana* is purely mental with the usual triads. THE AIM OF VICHARA IS FOR THE MIND IN ITS WAKING STATE TO REMAIN QUIESCENT, FOR STILLNESS IS THE SOLE REQUISITE FOR SELF-REALISATION. Hence *Vichara* is the direct method and not *Nididhyasana.* The latter may be an aid to *Vichara* in the initial stages. This is Sri Bhagavan's view.

He reiterates the direct method below:— "With vocal silence and mental quiescence and a completely indrawn mind to quest for the source of the 'I' is the direct method in *vichara marga.*" *Dhyana* of *Maha vakhyas* is a form of *mano vritti.* It cannot be mental *mowna*, hence mind cannot be one-pointed and dive deep. *The aim of vichara is annihilation of mind. It is not obtained by dhyana.* Howsoever long one may be practising *dhyana* it will not lead to annihilation of mind. Performing *dhyana*, mind can exist any length of time. The vital point in *vichara sadhana* is the mental determination to seek the source of the ego. This is not in *dhyana marga*. Sri Bhagavan says that *dhyana* is formed by the two words 'I' and 'That'. This double-headed *dhyana* is not helpful for the mind to dive deep. On the other hand *dhyana* of the single word 'I' is better.

Vichara is indicated by the two expressions "Who am I?" and "Whence am I?". The *sadhana* can be performed either way. "Who am I?" means which is the *Atma* and connotes the search for one's own Reality. "Whence am I?" means which is the source of the 'I thought', meaning the same search.

The fruit of this *sadhana* is JIVANMUKTHI.

OM TAT SAT

SRI RAMANARPANAMASTHU

APPENDIX B

Excerpts culled from the annotation to TRUTH REVEALED by 'Who', as expounded to him by Sri Bhagavan.

1. Grace turns the mind inward, links it with the Reality and thus destroys the ego, which is the 'I-am-the-body' idea.

2. *Brahman* is mindless, *i.e.*, thought-free.

3. So long as the ego is not destroyed all knowledge is ignorance (*ajnana*). The destruction of the 'I-thought' is knowledge.

4. An egoistic person is argumentative.

5. To get rid of the ego, the only method is to search for its source.

6. If the ego is destroyed, the self-effulgent, pure, eternal Self is realised without any hindrance.

7. Only to remain fixed in the Heart, devoid of thoughts, is meditation.

8. Introversion is nothing but the mind getting detached from the world and externals and getting fixed in the *sadhana*.

9. Unless extroversion is abandoned, it is impossible to introvert and concentrate.

10. *Vishnu* to Prahalada : "If you desire the deathless state, your *darsan* (sight) of me with your gross physical eye is not sufficient. You must have the sight of Vishnu inside you."

11. To get the mind introverted and to fix it with concentration on the Self (Heart) is *Atma Vichara.*

12. In the waking state the ego in the *vijnanamaya kosha* must be destroyed by *Atma Vichara.*

13. The mind getting introverted and searching for the source of the ego with concentration is the means for the mind to abide in the Self in the waking state.

14. Mind, so long as it does not turn inward and search for its source, will hinder Self-realisation.

15. Introverting in search of its source, the mind gets merged there and becomes thought-free; thereafter Self-realisation results.

16. The *jnana sadhana* or the practice for Self-realisation is for the in-turned mind to search for the source of the 'I-thought' with vocal silence and mental quiescence. The fruit of this is *jivanmukti.*

17. *Chittabhasa* always shines as 'I am this' (body). Consciousness of the Self always scintillates as 'I' 'I' meaning 'I am I'.

18. The phrase 'to know the Self' is to remain as the Self, *i.e.*, without thoughts.

19. In the deep sleep state, when the ego has subsided, the concepts of space and time are absent : so these are the products of the mind.

20. The world is nothing but name and form.

21. Of all the forms, that of the *Jnana Guru* is the holiest. That *Jnana Guru* must be regarded as the Supreme Being residing in the Heart. He who regards the Guru as distinct from the Supreme Self will never attain Self-realisation.